'I would like to dedicate this collection of poems to the people I have learnt to love, the people I have learnt to hate and the people I have learnt to forgive.'

-Tyler Reedman

Love/Hate Cherry Blossom

Contents

Skin

Softly damaged

Perfectly torn

Nurtured leather's

Barely worn

Virgin cloak

Fearing light

Whore's whispers

Lover's fight

Chronic

Burning out

Wearing thin

The bottom of the bottle

Where your life begins

Liver sore

Stomach pumped

The bottom of the stairs

Where your body lies slumped

Morning light

Aching head

Trying to remember

Remembering regret

Evening comes

You see a friend

Before it's even over

You've started it again

Ode to the obsessed

You make me smile

You make me cry

In you I'll live forever

In you I'll never die

You make me blossom

You make me decay

In you I'll find the reason

To live my final day

You make me heal

You make me cut

In you I find opportunity

In you all doors are shut

You make me burn

You make me freeze

In you I'll find the answers

When I'm begging on my knees

Regret the past

Wet skin on my skinny jeans

Fighting hard to live my teenage dream

I thought I'd drown in the depths of you

Instead I drowned in the drugs and booze

Fake it until you make it

You say you want to die

But did you try hard enough?

Not that I care to check

But I see your still here with us

You walked across the tracks

But did you walk far enough?

I really hate to ask

But why are you still here with us?

Party favours

Pretty pills

And time to kill

Tranquilize the way I feel

Blueish eyes

And fake surprise

Shot by the way she lies

No regrets

Living depressed

Shot by the way she dressed

Pretty pills

And time to kill

Freak show forever

I never meant to run away from myself

But I just can't bear to cry anymore

I never meant to stop loving myself

But I'm done with being society's whore

I never meant to make you wonder why

But I had no reason to let it out

I never meant to tell a lie

But no one understood what I was on about

So don't try to change

The world isn't a superstore

Society may give you your label

But you are worth so much more

Tears in July

Are you naked by yourself?

Do you dream of someone else?

Do you call her on your phone?

Do you want her all alone?

Are you searching for the truth?

Do your nightmares all come true?

Do you ever think of me?

Do you haunt me in my sleep?

Are you better than the rest?

Do you want my cigarette?

Do you want my embers too?

So you can rise up brand new

Do you want to hurt me?

Because your smile says otherwise

Will you hold me close?

Keep me trapped in your lies

And if you want to hurt me

And your smile does tell lies

Then just hold me close

When there are tears in July.

Some wounds heal

No theme

Nervous to be seen

Retreat

Let them make a scene

Your name

Once it meant something

Real shame

To me you are nothing

Reasonable doubt

Don't make me think of reasons

It's hard to go back there

Your crooked, ice cold treasons

The way you say you care

Our friendship still means nothing

I'm better than your spare

So lost looking for something

I'll find it in your stare

Love/hate cherry blossom

Sunshine on a cold winter's day

Rain on a perfect summer's night

When we run out of words to say

Can you blame us for wanting to fight?

Food in the starved child's mouth

Death at the rich man's door

When the world promised us everything

Could you blame us for asking for more?

Sweat on the politician's forehead

Fight in homeless man's eyes

When we kill all of our enemies

Who will we learn to despise?

Forgiveness is not a failure

Forgiveness is not a disgrace

Forgiveness is asking for better

Forgiveness is having good grace

Credit Card

Kill myself because I hate breathing

Cut you down because you're not special

I hope you feel this

Burn the pages because I hate memories

Re write the words because I'm not fabled

I hope you feel this

Light the match because you're no lighter

Breathe you in because you're not fragile

I hope I feel this

Tell the truth because I'm no liar

Put me down because I'm a hazard

I hope I feel this

Expand my pupils with some party powder

Kept it up because I'm not dead yet

Hope I feel this

Late that night I find myself in your bed

You remind me that I'm not special

Hope you feel this

~End~

Secrets

I wish to bath in the dirt of a secret

Plot to stab your back whilst I promise that I'll keep it

I wish to bath in the dirt of your lust

Work to hurt you deeply by breaking your trust

I want to know what you are feeling

Cut you out and hang your body from the ceiling

I want to know why you are broken

Cutting out your tongue for the secrets you have spoken

I need to know who you are inside

So I can find in you a place for me to hide

I need to know more than your name

So I can find in you a place for my shame

Printed in Great
Britain
by Amazon